THE AUSTRALIAN PROPERTY INVESTMENT HANDBOOK

2018–2019

E 7 STEPS YOU MUST FOLLOW
RY TIME YOU PURCHASE AN INVESTMENT PROPERTY

NDREW CROSSLEY

The Australian Property Investment Handbook

2018-19

2018-19

Andrew Crossley

First published by Busybird Publishing 2017

Copyright © 2017 Andrew Crossley

ISBN

Print: 978-1-925692-21-1
Ebook: 978-1-925692-22-8

Cover design: Luke Harris

Internal images: Caroline Ward; KiCreative and Nicole Ellingham; Love Ginger Designs.

Layout and typesetting: Busybird Publishing

Busybird Publishing
2/118 Para Road
Montmorency, Victoria
Australia 3094
www.busybird.com.au

busybird
publishing

Disclaimer

Contents

About this Book

This book takes you through the proven strategies and 7-step process that you must follow every time you purchase an investment property. It is based on my ground breaking 'Blueprint to success'. I designed my blueprint© to act as an easy to follow process to help as many people as possible achieve more success with property investment. This blueprint is a step by step process that I personally take my clients through as. It is written from the various perspectives of being one of Australia's leading buyer's agents/ property advisors and multi award winning Business Development Manager. You can obtain your free copy of this blueprint by going to www.australianpropertyadvisorygroup.com.au/resources and simply enter some details in order to access and download my blueprint. You will also have access to a 'readiness to invest' questionnaire and a very useful 'research checklist'.

Most investors get something wrong when buying a property, and when you look at why, 99% of the time it's because they did not follow every one of the seven steps in this book.

If you follow these seven steps, for every property purchase, you will save yourself time and money, dramatically reduce risk, improve potential, and almost certainly eliminate stress, frustration and fear from the experience.

There are also 'MUST' follow rules scattered throughout this book.

What you gain will be similar to you being mentored through

the process of not only knowing what to do when thinking about buying an investment property, but why you should do it.

Every successful investor assesses their situation and what they want to achieve. They establish a plan and they follow it, taking action to implement the plan. They undertake the required research and put in place finance strategies. They build a team around them to help them each step of the way toward their future income goals for retirement or an early retirement.

The steps in this book should function together, and many parts of each step (chapter) can be used/implemented simultaneously. To assist in a property being purchased in as much of a stress-free manner as possible, always refer to this book and if you wish to have further assistance, because you don't have time to do it yourself, or you are afraid or concerned with doing it yourself, it is recommended you contact www.australianpropertyadvisorygroup.com.au (APAG) to work with you each step of the way.

Also read:

Property Investing Made Simple

www.propertyinvestingmadesimple.com.au

Property Finance Made Simple

www.propertyfinancemadesimple.net.au

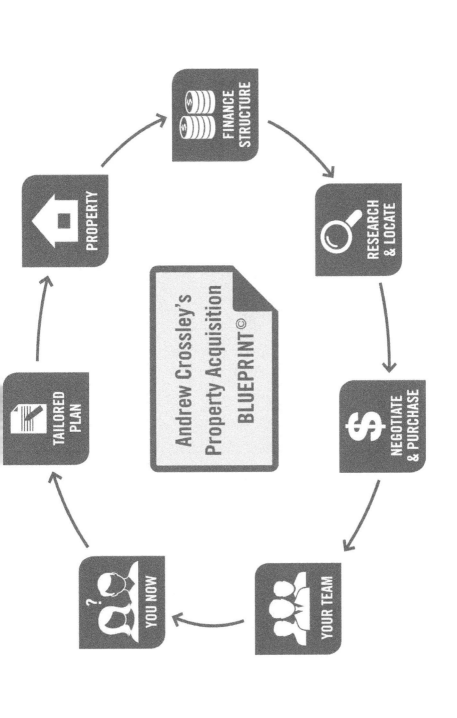

Andrew Crossley's
Property Acquisition
BLUEPRINT©

FINANCE STRUCTURE

RESEARCH & LOCATE

NEGOTIATE & PURCHASE

YOUR TEAM

YOU NOW

TAILORED PLAN

PROPERTY

About the Author

Andrew Crossley lives in Melbourne, and is the #1 best-selling and award-winning author of two books.

Property Investing Made Simple

www.propertyinvestingmadesimple.com.au

and *Property Finance Made Simple*

www.propertyfinancemadesimple.net.au.

Andrew has worked in the finance and property industry for over 21 years, 12 of those years in Australia, including working for the largest non-bank/largest mortgage manager during that time, and has worked overseas in private wealth management on several continents.

Andrew is a partner in the 'Australian Property Advisory Group' (APAG) www.apag.com.au. APAG was a finalist in the Australian small business awards of 2016.

Property Industry Awards include:

- Finalist: Best Buyer's Agent in Australia in the Readers' Choice Awards (Highly Recommended) 2016
- Runner Up: Best Buyer's Agent in Australia: Readers' Choice Awards 2015
- Highly Recommended: Investors Choice awards 2015: Buyer's Agent
- Highly Recommended: Investors Choice awards 2015: Property Investment Advisor

Finance Industry Awards include:

- •• NATIONAL WINNER: Mortgage and Finance Association of Australia (MFAA) 2017
- •• STATE WINNER: Mortgage and Finance Association of Australia (MFAA) 2017
- •• Finalist: Better Business Awards 2017
- •• Finalist: Mortgage and Finance Association of Australia (MFAA) 2016
- •• Finalist: Mortgage and Finance Association of Australia (MFAA) 2015
- •• Finalist: Mortgage and Finance Association of Australia (MFAA) 2014
- •• Finalist: Australia Mortgage Association 2016
- •• Finalist: Australia Mortgage Association 2015

Book awards and milestones:

Property Investing Made Simple

- •• #1 Best seller
- •• Best book: in 'Real Estate' International book awards 2015
- •• Best book: in 'Real Estate' Book excellence awards 2016
- •• In stores and libraries around Australia now

Property Finance Made Simple

- •• #1 Best seller and #67 in all books on Amazon Kindle Australia,
- •• In all good book stores

The Australian Property Investment Handbook 2018/19

The 100k Property Plan (how to earn 100k per year from property) … coming soon.

Qualifications include:

- •• Accredited Property Investment Advisor PIPA
- •• Qualified Property Inv. Advisor (QPIA)
- •• Fully licensed Real Estate Agent (NSW, VIC, QLD)
- •• Advanced Diploma in Financial Services (Financial Planning)
- •• Diploma in Finance (Mortgage Broking Management)
- •• Masters in Business Administration
- •• Masters in Commerce
- •• Masters in Commercial Law

Andrew has also written for dozens of industry and non-industry publications and appeared on TV and radio. He is an educator, mentor, consultant and public speaker.

Having grown a personal portfolio of over 10 properties, consisting of houses, townhouses, dual occupancies and units across several states, Andrew was recognised in the 'Your Investment Property Magazine' Property Investor Awards 2012.

Personal Message:

I am sure you will enjoy reading my book as much as I have enjoyed writing it and sharing my knowledge and insights with you.

Whether buying your first investment property or your next, it should be a worthwhile and enjoyable experience.

1

Your current situation

With anything you do of importance in life, it is far better to understand what you need to do before you try and do it. Without hope and goals we merely exist, there is nothing to strive for or look forward to. Having a goal gives direction and purpose in life, be it a small or big goal, short term or long term.

In terms of property investment, your main goal should be a monetary one, NOT 'I want 10 properties in 10 years'. This is foolish, dumb, and it lacks a practical outcome. The reason for the goal can be anything, such as a legacy, dream holiday or comfortable retirement. In retirement, life comes down to survival and you need money for that.

A useful and considered outcome comes from determining your income requirement in retirement.

Retirement age can be open-ended; for some people it could be earlier in life than others. The younger someone starts investing, the more time for those assets to grow in value, and the more income potential will be derived from those assets in retirement.

Many people tend to assume that if they work hard and save money then one day they will end up wealthy. This is wishful thinking for most people, as 80% will end up on the pension. With this mind-set, they are more likely to end up with a modest but ultimately less useful amount of savings. They are unlikely to be wealthy unless they have their own business and sell it for a couple of million dollars.

An income figure could be $40,000 or $200,000 pa; what matters is that the figure is right for you. Once you have a goal you will need to work backwards and knowing what you want and need in your retirement, it is easier to establish a plan of action. When you are still young and working, it is easier to leverage on your assets, in particular property, whilst not overstretching yourself. You still need to have a life.

Once you have a goal, you need to consider your current situation. There is no point having a goal that is completely unachievable. What is achievable can often be more than what you might think, though, if you have a good team around you.

Income:

Your income will determine how much you can borrow. It also forms part of what you can afford to spend and save, and it impacts on what you can contribute to an investment property.

Assets and Liabilities:

The amount of debt you have will also impact on what you can borrow. The more credit cards you have, the worse off your borrowing capacity is.

Your age:

This will impact on your ability to obtain a loan, especially if you are over 55. The main impact from a property perspective is that it will directly impact how much time you have left to work and to achieve your 'passive income' goal for retirement. It will also impact on the viable length of the plan moving forward, and the level of risk appropriate for your situation.

Your living expenses:

This impacts on the level of debt you can afford, your borrowing capacity, and the amount you can save. Lenders are placing an ever-increasing significance on this. In fact, besides your income, this is one of the greatest variables, and every lender treats your living expenses differently.

Your surplus/spare money:

This will contribute to what the plan needs to look like, and what is possibly achievable. If you need to purchase a capital growth focused property, then often by default it will be negatively geared, and you would need to afford the higher out-of-pocket cost. The Government has now intentionally made it more difficult for you to afford to buy an established property, given you can no longer claim any depreciation on any fixtures and fittings that came with the property.

Risk appetite and profile:

Investing involves risk. Risk is the chance that an investment will not give you the returns you hoped for. You could lose money or not make any money. All investments have risk, but some have more than others.

Generally, investments that are expected to pay higher returns involve more risk. These investments are likely to produce higher returns over time than more conservative investments. Over short periods of time investments can fall in value. Property is a long-term, not short-term investment, unless you plan to develop or renovate the property. With a buy and hold strategy, it's certainly a long-term strategy.

Your risk profile when determining a property plan is not designed to determine if you should invest in property or another asset, it's used to determine the strategy within the scope of property investment. Each type of strategy, location and property has its own risks and benefits. Your risk profile can be used to assist with trying to choose a strategy and property more suited to you.

If you want a positive cash flow property this tends to suit lower risk appetites, preferring not to take the risk of being too negatively geared or the risk of waiting 10-15 years for an increase in value. Perhaps your health or job security is such that you prefer not to be out of pocket too much. Capital growth strategies require a slightly higher risk appetite as you have to wait for the growth, whilst earning less from the property.

Some people may be more aggressive or assertive in how they wish to move forward, sometimes from desperation, or out of sheer necessity. However, a plan forward needs to be justified and responsible, managing your expectations, and avoiding becoming a slave to your debt. Sometimes a risk appetite does not correlate to a risk profile. For example, a couple who has more than 2-3 credit cards are a higher-risk profile, but may have a very low risk appetite.

Some 'would be' property investors have a higher risk appetite than what they should have for their circumstances. This can end up putting them in a precarious situation, being exposed to too much debt, and an untenable future cost of debt.

Needs will vary depending on experience, knowledge and risk profile. Less experienced buyers generally want someone to manage the process for them, and help them find a property.

Rule:

Always have a SMART goal. It must be specific, measurable, attainable, relevant to you and focused on a fixed point in time.

To fill in a readiness to invest questionnaire, please go to www.australianpropertyadvisorygroup.com.au/resources

In Summary: Your age, income, borrowing capacity, living expenses, surplus money and risk profile will all have a bearing on the plan, and the reality and likelihood of the outcome (viability of your goal). Compromises may need to be made.

No two people will have the same strategy – it may be similar, but not the same. Your future is in your hands and you need to own it. Be responsible for it so that you can enjoy your future, just as you intended or hoped it to be.

2

Tailored Plan

Fear, not purchasing well, not building a large enough property portfolio, or simply just buying a property or two with no idea what the properties should be, all affect a goal being achieved.

An intelligent investor will not just focus on capital growth. They want to avoid the risk of becoming a slave to their portfolio, to have to keep working just to make repayments thinking they will wake up in 10 years and the portfolio has doubled. They want to sleep at night as interest rates rise (and they are, and will continue to independently of the RBA).

An intelligent investor will not focus just on positive cash flow either, as they want to achieve capital growth and more wealth at retirement. Whilst they don't want their properties to be a negative impact on their lifestyle, they realise the importance of capital growth.

Too many authors of property investment books, and others that operate within the property industry, promote just one strategy: either capital growth in blue chip suburbs or positive cash flow in regional locations. This is misguided.

The most optimal plan is to buy several capital growth properties with excellent cash flow in blue chip suburbs near major infrastructure hubs, preferably near Melbourne or Sydney CBD.

The reality is not everyone can afford to do this. The idealists out there who promote only buying capital growth properties in blue chip suburbs, or only buying positive cash flow focused properties, are just that – they are idealists, not realists. Their logic, in isolation to most people's financial situations, is sound, but it is disconnected from the vast reality of society in general, of typical mum and dad investors in the burbs.

Good capital growth locations typically have low yield. This would mean the property would likely be negatively geared.

Cash flow focused properties are in areas with less capital growth. At least this strategy reduces the risk of being exposed too much to the unknown future cost of debt. Fixing your interest rates can help as well, providing knowledge of what your repayments will be for a while. But no one can beat the banks – in the long term it works out to roughly the same as having a variable rate loan.

RULE:

Investors need a balance of both capital growth and cash flow in order to grow a portfolio and more likely achieve their goal.

Most investors do not earn enough to afford to buy 5-7 properties in blue chip suburbs without regard for cash flow from those properties. Most people do not earn 200k+ a year, their job stability is not 10 out of 10, they do have fear, and lack knowledge and experience. People need help to invest in a practical way to suit them and their specific needs, not an ideological single strategy fashion, bereft of suitability and sustainability to them.

Cash flow properties are not necessarily wealth creation properties. They do, however, provide greater income while you are growing your portfolio, therefore allowing a property investor an increased capacity to continue to borrow. If the focus is only on capital growth properties, the ability to continue to borrow money will diminish, ultimately; they would run out of income to service the loans. If an investor could no longer borrow money, it would not matter how much equity they have, as they'd be unable to access it.

It would be too easy, and very wrong to base a decision on just one property. There are several considerations to bear in mind. Besides your exposure to the future cost of debt and receiving tax deductions, affordability to purchase more properties – whilst enabling you to continue to reduce your mortgage on your home – is very important. Combined, they provide hope; hope toward a brighter retirement, having done something rather than nothing.

The risk with only a capital growth strategy is the amount the borrower could be out of pocket while holding the properties. In a rising interest rate market (rates for investment loans) the risk grows.

There's no point buying a capital growth focused property if there is a clear and present risk that in the near future the property will need to be sold. Job uncertainty, tightening lending policies, lower borrowing capacity and risk of having to sell the property due to unforeseen circumstances is much higher. Changes to negative gearing are already problematic with established properties.

In one report by J.P Morgan, it was revealed that finance for more property purchases was no longer possible for up to 10% of 'would be' investors.

Lenders used to account for borrower's existing debt with other lenders by using actual repayments to determine the borrower's cost of debt. On an interest only loan of 500k in 2016, the repayments might have been $22,500 pa. Now, lenders are adding a buffer on top of the borrowing capacity calculator, and converting the interest only repayments to a figure based on principle and interest, as they always have done for the new loan being applied for.

The same 500k debt in 2017 would have a cost associated to it of $41,500 pa, based not just on a higher qualifying rate but also principle and interest repayments, even though the investor may be paying interest only.

This is $19,000 more in income the borrowers need to have to afford the same debt on a bank's calculator as they previously could have.

Imagine they only purchased capital growth properties and none of them were cash flow focused properties, the strife this investor would be in, and on two main fronts.

- Not being able to borrow as much and/or

- Maybe being forced to sell one or more, due to rising rates, and rising holding cost of debt

Many investors over the years have been drawn to negative gearing, yet it makes less sense why these people were. Of course, they think they are saving a great deal of tax but let's put this into perspective.

According to the ATO, over 70% of investors that have a negatively geared property (a property not breaking even or not making positive cash flow) earn under 80k per annum. So their tax bracket is mid-range, not high, or the highest. So it is really foolish to spend a dollar just to save 32.5 cents and this is what **all** these people are doing that earn under 80k per annum.

There are three strategies for property investors;

Capital growth and cash flow strategies can be implemented in all three. The difference between the three of them is level of risk, time available to retirement, your tailored plan, comfort level, and many other influences.

1. Buy and hold

This is perhaps the easiest of the three strategies. It is more suited to time poor investors that wish to be a little more conservative, or that lack the knowledge and expertise to risk undertaking one of the other two strategies. Buy and hold is what the majority of investors decide on.

Many still fail with this for innumerable reasons. Lack of knowledge and experience, poor research, not using an advisor, bad financial strategy, no plan, selling too early, buying at the wrong time in the wrong market, or buying the wrong property type in a good suburb.

2. Flipping or holding by renovating

This requires a more hands-on approach or paying a premium to have someone renovate for you. The purchaser can manufacture more capital growth and cash flow independently of the market, so they're not solely reliant on the market for the property's performance. If too much emotion is involved and they over-capitalise, serious problems will arise. Having it vacant for an extended period while work is being carried out means being out of pocket for a period of time. Affordability could then be an issue, as it is more difficult to afford to have a property vacant for an extended period.

3. Develop

This includes construction of another dwelling or several dwellings on the block, and/or subdivision. This is the most risky, due to time and cost, but has potential for significantly more financial benefits from a cash flow and capital growth perspective. A feasibility study would be required to determine if the project will make enough money or will lose money. You will also need a good team around you. Refer to www.propertyinvestingmadesimple.com.au to get an idea of who would be needed in your team for this type of investment. Also stay tuned for my next book, 'The 100k Property Plan' where I go into significant detail on everything to do with small-scale developments.

With every plan, there are also three stages

1. An acquisition phase:

This is the period of time over which you acquire the required properties. It can be as short or long as is practical, but needs to suit your current situation and all the elements of what makes up your current situation discussed in chapter 1.

2. The holding phase:

This is the period of time that you hold your properties. The longer this phase, with a buy and hold strategy, the more time the properties have to grow in value. Many property-marketing companies will tell you that property has doubled in value every 7-10 years and whilst this is true in many areas, what these people do wrong is imply that property will continue to double the next 7-10 years. They may not say it explicitly, but they often lead you to believe the chances of it are very high.

This I disagree with; the past is not a reliable indicator of the future. To be more reasonable with timeframes and in order to manage expectations, it is more reliable to allow 15 years, or even 20 years is better. Not everyone has this much time, and it is a sad fact of life that people leave it too late in life to take action for the betterment of their future. What can be done for people who are young enough, is to consider starting now if your current situation allows it. For those people who have left it late, they could also consider whether they should start now, to at least try and improve their situation, and seek advice at least.

The older someone becomes, the more conservative they should consider being. They have less time to try and mitigate any financial mistakes they make.

3. Exit phase:

There are five main exit strategies. It is best to seek advice from a property advisor for a tailored approach.

1. Sell some and pay off the debt on the rest leaving the remaining properties hopefully unencumbered. This works when there are more than just a few properties, and some with a capital growth focus. You may or may not have reduced some of the debt. The less debt you want to reduce, the more confidence you would need with the market.

2. Reduce your debt, assisted by an offset account and principle and interest (P & I) repayments on any mortgage against your principle place of residence (PPR). Firstly, focus on the debt not providing any tax benefit. Once non-deductible debt is paid off, then consider an offset against the deductible debt against the principle place of residence, or investment property, originally used for deposit and costs of a property purchase.

3. A blend of 1 and 2 is probably optimal unless all debt can be paid off from personal endeavour (working for a living).

4. Live off equity in retirement. Prior to retiring, apply to refinance all properties, setting up redraw or line of credit against some or all. Using equity to live off is different to earning income to live off, as it is not taxed.

5. Sell all properties. Hopefully walk away with two million in equity, then purchase a few properties with really high yield, for example 10% and live off the rent.

Example: If your home, or preferably an investment property, had enough equity to establish a line of credit/redraw against it of $400k (could be more, but let's say $400k), just before retirement, while still earning assumedly sufficient income to service this amount.

The undrawn equity could sit in the loan not incurring interest. It could provide $40k pa to live off for 10 years, which would put the borrower in the top percentage of retired income earners in Australia.

Let's assume superannuation and any additional shares provide an income of $15k pa. Only $25k needs to be used from the line of credit/redraw to earn $40k per year, meaning the $400k in redraw could last for 16 years. Imagine having a couple of properties with access to $400k equity in each.

Note: the point number four is one some others promote. It has, as a concept, been around for 20 years, but often these people fail to adequately explain the mechanics and downside of it. Some reasons it may be problematic are:

1. Accessing equity after retirement is very difficult and unlikely possible, as lenders will need the borrower to have enough income to service an increase in the existing debt level, and an acceptable exit strategy.
2. Lending policy may inhibit further borrowing; you cannot rely on what lenders will do in five, or 25 years. Additionally, it is not always so easy to refinance just when the borrower wants to.
3. You will eventually die, leaving all the debt-covered properties to someone else. This would be unfortunate and not considered a welcomed legacy.
4. Some elderly decide on a reverse mortgage, and this does have serious consequences. It's one of the most expensive forms of debt, may leave the person unable to afford aged care, and it may affect pension eligibility.

In summary: The type of property strategies and the number of properties of each strategy will impact on location choice, and therefore outcome. Between 5-7 well purchased properties is better than just choosing a number like 10 as a naïve goal for your portfolio. Property advisors do have software to model outcomes using conservative assumptions of growth and yield figures.

It is important that you don't just buy and then sit and wait. You need to review your plan, portfolio, goals based on any changes to your circumstances, and the performance of the property and the market which it's in. Using conservative figures will manage your expectations. It means that if the portfolio performs better, you may exceed what you had planned for. If it does not perform as well as you might anticipate, at least you have been conservative. Also review your risk tolerance.

Reducing debt that provides tax deductions is not the best approach if you have debt that does not provide you tax deductions, but it does have other benefits, which need to be weighed up. Whilst any applicable depreciation on the dwelling is on a straight-line method at 2.5% each year over

40 years, depreciation on fittings and fixtures, if applicable, does diminish over the short term, so the cost of debt will increase accordingly. To help mitigate this rise in cost of debt (to help weather the storm of rising rates) especially on interest only and investment loans, and to maximum the difference between the value of the property and level of debt, and make it more cash flow positive (if you can afford to), a debt reduction strategy is generally wise.

The bigger picture is the focus here, in a managed manner of course, but if you significantly reduce your debt over time, it will lessen the debt ultimately against your properties and perhaps reduce the number of properties you may need to sell. It's very important to consider principle and interest repayments on the properties.

Rule:

Please remember you will probably have to convert your repayments to principle and interest at some point, which in turn will reduce your debt. The more debt you do reduce, the better the outcome in the end, as long as you can afford to do this.

You need capital growth for wealth creation. This can provide the equity which may be accessed to use for the deposit and costs of buying more properties, paying off debt on other properties nearer retirement leaving a final number unencumbered. Paul Clitheroe from *Money Magazine* proposes a multiple of 17. Work out what you need in retirement, and then multiply it by 17, this is what you will apparently need. He suggests that 17 is the years you will live beyond retirement. If you live beyond that, well, you are in trouble. If you retire too early, then you may also be in trouble.

A plan's focus is to acquire an appropriate number of properties for your specific needs, over a given time, at a given price, to achieve a desired passive income – all within an appropriate risk tolerance and level of affordability throughout the entire process.

It is worth reiterating that a plan is better than not having a plan at all. If you fall short, well, you would have achieved more than not having a plan to begin with.

My next book will go much more in-depth and provide examples of tailored plans, so stay tuned.

3

Property Strategy

Once you have a plan of action, it is important to determine the type of properties that best suit the chosen path forward. The order in which you implement the plan will be clear if it's well written.

The first choice you need to make is between Residential and Commercial property. This book will focus more on residential. My next book will include a great deal of depth on commercial finance and commercial property, and what you need to know.

RULE:

Negative gearing is NOT a strategy; never focus on buying a negatively geared property.

Negative gearing is simply a bi-product of a property purchase that is not cash flow positive from the get go, more commonly referred to as a bi-product of capital growth. To build a portfolio, people are wrong to think they should choose to avoid negative gearing or include negative gearing in their plan.

The loan to value ratio (LVR), more specifically your level of debt versus the value of the property, and the cost of that debt versus income coming in from the property, will determine if the property is negatively geared.

Any property can end up being positively geared, it just depends on what you're able to do to it, such as renovate or subdivide. For properties with less scope for development or manufacturing more value or yield, a debt reduction strategy will help.

Now: The question you should ask yourself is how best to move forward?

The answer is you must maximise your outcome while also maximising your on-going borrowing capacity and equity/

cash position, while having a balance with your current lifestyle.

If you are focused too heavily on capital growth you will negatively impact on your borrowing capacity, as capital growth strategies often require a compromise on yield/cash flow, which mean you will earn less from the property while you own it (ignoring some potential benefits from renovating or developing).

If you earn less on a property than what you could on another property, the holding cost is higher. It could affect you, your family, your budget, and your ability to enjoy life now. You could become a slave to your debt, forever forced to work just to afford the debt. This vicious cycle is best avoided.

Some authors of investment property books promote positive cash flow strategies as being better than capital growth strategies and vice versa. They often forget that the average investor is not in a position to just focus on one and not the other.

In retirement, it is obvious you need income or a source of money. It is important to have some excellent cash flow producing properties, whilst it is as equally important to not have too much debt, thus avoiding the 'cost of the debt' mitigating the benefit of the potential positive cash flow nature of the properties.

Whether you are starting out or midway through your property journey, or nearer retirement, you continually need to assess your options of how geared you wish to be. Starting out on your journey may require you to borrow to a higher amount (LVR) as you may not have much saved or have not accumulated any capital growth in any assets. Later on in life you hopefully would have built up some equity and/or saved some cash.

A higher price property could expose you to being out of your comfort zone and if the property is vacant, you have a larger debt to cover. If the price is lower and you spread any borrowing capacity over several properties, you can reduce this risk, but it would also limit the dollar figure of growth associated with the property.

For example: A million-dollar property grows 10%. This equals $100k capital growth. If a $500k property grows in 10% in value, this is $50k capital growth. Conversely, if there is an 80% debt against the million-dollar property i.e. $800k, and for some reason it is vacant, you have a super large debt to make repayments on. If a $500k property has an 80% debt (i.e. $400k) and it happens to be vacant, you have a much more affordable debt or cost of debt to make repayments on.

In general, a lower priced property has better yield than a higher priced property. Having more properties around the $400-600k price will produce more rental yield (percentage, not in dollar terms) than the same number of $1-2 million of properties.

Comparison of a unit versus apartment versus a townhouse, versus a house.

You cannot always compare these as easily as you may like. A well-purchased unit will outperform an averagely purchased house. After all your research, you can compare the performance of a suburb within your budget and the past growth of specific sized dwellings very easily. Units, apartments and townhouses often offer better proximity to amenities and transport, and are more affordable than a house in the same suburb. Units and townhouses provide higher yield, the owners corporation covers building insurance, whereas, normally with a house, you will pay this yourself.

Note: Some master planned estates are popping up and the houses in some of these estates do have owner corporation costs as well. It is no longer just units, apartments and some townhouses that have owner's corporation costs.

Units offer lower maintenance, apartments offer little to no garden for the tenant to manage, and common ground is the responsibility of the owner's corporation, not the owner.

Units, townhouses and apartments offer 'would be' investors a more affordable way into the property market.

Townhouses are often a great compromise for a budget, they are between a unit and a house. They will not grow as much as a house in the same suburb but they may be better than a unit in the same suburb, and better than an apartment in the same suburb.

The least of them all is apartments; they have less land on title than a unit. A unit sits on its own bit of land, an apartment sits in a building with other apartments. Except for those on the ground floor, apartments do not sit on their own plot of land. They simply have a percentage allocation of the land the whole building sits on, a very watered-down value compared to a unit, townhouse or house.

I would not buy an apartment close to Melbourne CBD at the moment, with a looming 50,000-apartment oversupply. Same for Brisbane, developers have ravaged the landscape and skyline; many suburbs are simply plagued with apartments. If you can, consider buying a unit, townhouse or house in high-density suburbs especially, but elsewhere as well.

Units and townhouses may have perhaps 150-300 sqm of land they sit on, with units being single story and townhouses double story (main difference).

The next diagram demonstrates the difference between buying an older house versus a new townhouse. They are assumed to be the same price in the same suburb, the house has more land, and the house would not have much value, so the sale price would be roughly the same as a brand new townhouse. A townhouse would have less land, but most of the value is in the dwelling. You will see that even though buying a house will provide more capital growth in this realistic example, it will limit you as to the amount of wealth the investor could afford to create, as the cost of owning the portfolio would be prohibitive.

Purchasing a townhouse as a once off property will provide less growth than a house in the same area for the same price, but it would allow more properties to be purchased, therefore more wealth to be created over time.

Here is the crucial process of sourcing a good property

	ESTABLISHED HOUSE	NEW TOWNHOUSE
Price	600k	600k
Land Size	550sqm	290sqm
Capital Growth	8.50%	5.50%
Stamp Duty	30k	8k
Rent	$440	$460
Interest Rate	4.50%	4.50%
Interest repayment type	I/O	I/O
Rental expenses* including rates, agents commission, letting fee, landlord and/or building insurance, maintenance, bodycorporate	30%	24%
Depreciation on Building	0	yes
Depreciation on fittings and fixtures	0	yes
Income (wage) of investor	90k	90k
Tax saving year 1	4.9k	8.87k
Holding cost per week^	$148	$33

	ESTABLISHED HOUSE	NEW TOWNHOUSE
Number of properties owned in 10 years	1	4
Price of other purchases	0	550k x 3
In 10 years, the compounded value in the example is	1.357 million	4.9 million

Some points worth noting on this example are:

1. Differences include no body corporate on the house, so building and contents insurance $1200, on the townhouse, there is body corporate of $1200, which does include building insurance. Landlord insurance $250. Maintenance for a new townhouse, say $500 a year at the start. Established property say $2,000 a year at the start.

2. The cost of $33 per week to own one townhouse will make it considerably easier for an investor to afford, and it is assumed it will make it easier to then buy more. In this example, I have used three more properties. Four properties at $33 a week costing around the same as just one established property.

3. Let's assume the second property was purchased in year two, the third property in year five and the fourth property in year seven. The figures represent the combined compound growth of these four properties, versus just the one house.

4. The investor would have 4.9 million versus 1.37 million, if they only considered the attributed of a property in isolation to a longer-term plan. Big mistake to look at each property in isolation to the bigger picture.

Rule:

Always do the best you can with what you have, it is almost always better to invest wisely than not invest at all.

Rule:

Always consider the value of the land as a component of the purchase price and value.

Land size is less important than the value of the land for the size it is. In other words, 200sqm of land within 10km of the CBD of Melbourne is worth much, much, much more than two acres of land in some suburbs 60km from the CBD, and worth more than 600sqm of land in a regional area.

Never fall for the trap of buying a house, when you hear that houses perform better than units without realising that it depends where and what you are comparing.

Residential property falls into four broad types.

Type 1: Unwanted, to be avoided.

For purposes of comparison, let's rule out the less desirable stuff.

1. Serviced apartments.
2. Student accommodation.
3. Buildings of apartments with over 75 apartments in a capital city.
4. Buildings with more than 10-15 apartments in a regional location (non-metropolitan location).
5. Buildings with lifts, as body corporate fees are higher, eating into rental income.
6. Buildings with pools, same as previous point.
7. Resorts.
8. Properties with limitations written into the owner corporation terms and conditions, limitations and exclusions can negatively impact on you, the rent ability and the future of your investment. Examples can include, no pets, short term lease restrictions on things such as Airbnb can apply, eliminating you from renting it out to short stay tenants. Improvements: You will be limited to what you can do, you do own the living space but not the walls, or car spot, or doors. You cannot add much value, if any, to an apartment. Rogue management: unreasonable or excessive increases in owner's corporation fees are a risk, and you the owner pays this, not the tenant.
9. Dwellings under 50 sqm living.

10. Apartments in some high-density postcodes, 3000-3009 for example, unless they are especially boutique, and not part of a high rise. Of course, this philosophy of avoidance is not related to apartments for you to live in, it is purely in relation to whether you want your investment to rent easily, sell easily should you ever want to, and grow in value. If you want to self-sabotage, go ahead and invest in Southbank or Docklands in Melbourne.

11. Dwellings on major roads, within 50 metres of high tension power lines.

Type 2: Unit, apartment, townhouse, house, villa. Most investors purchase these standard types of properties to buy and hold.

Type 3: Dual occupancy: Some growth and great yield. There are a few boxes that can be ticked here. A) Growth potential, though this will vary, not 6% growth, B) Yield, % yield in relation to price is better in some places than others, the higher the price the lower the yield. C) Price point, D) Manufacture capital growth potential sometimes, by separating the titles (community title).

Type 4: Properties that tick all four boxes of price combined with potential, yield, market growth, and manufacture growth with subdivision is development with some of the types of properties listed under type 2. Not so much a buy and hold strategy in this instance.

As time progresses the purchase price is assumed to go up, so the more spread out the acquisition phase of this plan the more you will probably pay for each property. A property now, in a given suburb, will be more expensive in the same suburb in five years typically. Dilemma; buying more properties in a shorter time to keep price lower versus buying them over a longer period, for comfort and affordability reasons, and paying more for them. Any time a client shortens the acquisition phase and lengthens the holding phase, they're maximising the holding period to achieve better results.

Should You Buy a New or Older Investment Property?

The higher rent, likely less repairs and maintenance, higher desirability for a tenant, lower stamp duty, lower holding cost, more depreciation, greater affordability to build a portfolio, and builder warranty, combined with any negative aspects of some new property, could still equal or be better than an established dwelling.

An established dwelling with lower rent, less desirability for tenants and higher repairs and maintenance risk, higher stamp duty, higher holding cost, less to no depreciation, with no builder warranty, but capital growth, won't normally be as good with new property.

Valuations not stacking up with new property is a risk. Claiming the depreciation is not the gilded lily many people think. It simply makes the holding cost of the property more affordable until sale.

Benefits of New Property

1. If you wish to reduce risk of repairs and maintenance, then new is handier.
2. Light and space are maximised.
3. They usually offer more depreciation benefits, investors can use these tax benefits to assist with monthly cash flow.
4. Stamp duty savings.

Disadvantages of New Property

1. You pay a premium compared to older properties in the same area.
2. Too many similar properties being sold at the same time; depending where.
3. Difficult to add value by renovating or extending.

New Property Valuations

Things that may not be considered in a valuation:

1. Level of finish/quality, better quality means the construction contract price is higher.
2. Lack of comparable sales in the location. Developer sales are not considered acceptable comparable sales.
3. Values not understanding the product i.e. dual occupancy.
4. GST; lenders are starting to deduct this from the sale price.

Refer to

www.propertyinvestingmadesimple.com.au

to understand more about house and land style contracts, and off the plan.

Benefits of Older Property

1. More chance to negotiate.
2. You can potentially add instant value through renovating, extending, subdividing and/or developing.
3. Older properties are often situated on larger blocks, which usually drives property value upwards.
4. Better if found in well-established suburbs, which can demonstrate consistent growth.

Disadvantages of Older Property

1. Lower rental rates.
2. Higher maintenance costs.
3. Lower depreciation.
4. Higher holding costs.

4

Finance

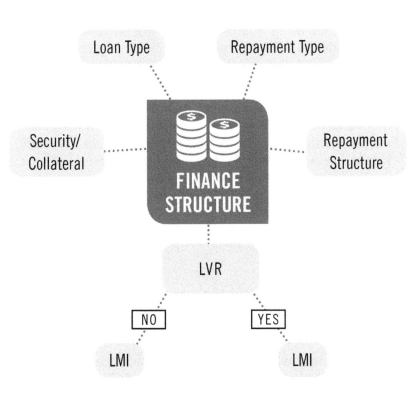

Rule:

Avoid using a company that is vertically integrated, i.e. they have their own finance division, property division and even conveyancing division, there are too many horror stories to mention that have resulted from people using these types of organisations. There is quite simply a complete lack of accountability if everything is done in house.

When considering buying an investment property, the most important thing you need to know is what you can afford to borrow. Until you know this you cannot start looking for a property, unless you just want to waste your time.

I recommend using a broker. There are so many reasons why you should not go straight to a bank. My recent book is a must read for you to understand this more. www. propertyfinancemadesimple.net.au.

Bank branches can place a great deal of pressure on their 'in house' loan writers, expecting them to cross sell insurance, financial planning services and other types of debt like credit cards and personal loans. As recent events have demonstrated, even the biggest banks can be investigated for scandals, selling the wrong insurance products to the wrong people, and end up investigated by the regulatory authorities for alleged involvement in money laundering activities.

Rule:

When obtaining finance, do not go directly to a bank; use a good broker.

When assessing what is best suited to your needs, you need to consider the loan type and features such as line of credit, a redraw facility, an offset account, a fixed rate loan, length of time to fix the loan, variable rate loan, and whether you pay lenders mortgage insurance.

Every lender is different as are their borrowing capacity calculators. Your borrowing capacity may vary by tens and tens of thousands.

The cost of the mortgage should never be based just on current interest rates, but rather the future cost of debt. Look at 'repayment figure' not 'interest rate' to understand the cost to you.

There are many cases where a lower rate can equal higher repayments, compared to a slightly higher rate with lower repayments, due to lower fees. The most important consideration is whether the loan gives you what you want, this is determined by policy, whether the policy of that particular lender ticks all your boxes. It is a minefield out there and can be quite frustrating doing it yourself.

Most people focus on the 'now', not the 'what if'. The modelling of holding costs – taking into account interest rates, lending criteria, income being earned, unexpected changes in personal circumstances – and being better prepared, is so important. Not factoring in the potential future cost of debt in conjunction with actual living expenses (which may differ to the standard expenses the lender will factor in), is the craziest thing you can do.

Deciding when to fix or have your rate variable

Ultimately, it's a question of risk appetite. If a person has a low risk appetite, perhaps fixed rates are important. It is not necessarily about making or saving money as much as it is about minimising future risk.

Variable rates used to be tied to the market but they're now at regular and on-going 'risk' at being changed as and when, and to what, the given lender feels in the mood for at the time, especially for interest only on investment and owner-occupied loans and principle and interest repayments on investment, although to a lesser degree.

To hedge your bets, perhaps you consider half fixed and half variable; it's a personal decision.

Fixing the rate is a risk reduction strategy. It provides piece of mind that for the selected period of time the interest rate won't change and the repayment will stay the same. Bear in mind the lender has priced the fixed rate to the projected market, meaning they have more resources than you or me – and you cannot outsmart them.

Principal and Interest (P&I)

These loans have higher repayments than interest-only loans, as some of the repayment is going toward reducing the loan principal (debt amount) over the life of the loan. At the start of the usual 30-year loan term the majority of the repayment is interest, but over time, the principle component increases as a component of the repayment. You will note in the next diagram, the amount of interest saved on a principle and interest loan, roughly $237,000

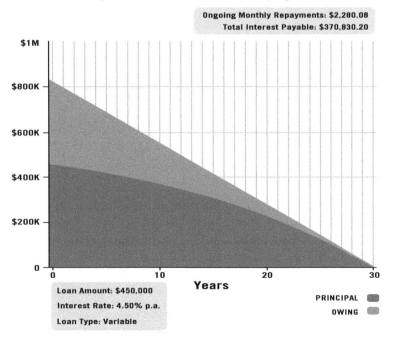

Principle & Interest Loan Repayments

Ongoing Monthly Repayments: $2,280.08
Total Interest Payable: $370,830.20

Loan Amount: $450,000
Interest Rate: 4.50% p.a.
Loan Type: Variable

PRINCIPAL
OWING

Interest-Only (I/O)

For a period of time, usually five years to 10 years, the borrower only has to make interest repayments on the mortgage, and does not need to pay back any of the money borrowed during this period. Investors have traditionally applied to the same lender or refinanced to a different lender to continue to only have interest only repayments, thinking that they will worry about paying back the debt in 30 year's time, or certainty not in the next 10-20 years. This is a big mistake. See the next example of the difference in interest you will pay over 30 years with an interest only loan versus a principle and interest loan, roughly $237,000 more interest will be paid from you to the lender.

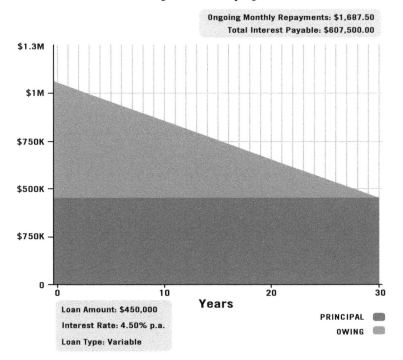

Interest Only Loan Repayments

Ongoing Monthly Repayments: $1,687.50
Total Interest Payable: $607,500.00

Loan Amount: $450,000
Interest Rate: 4.50% p.a.
Loan Type: Variable

PRINCIPAL
OWING

Years

Yes, the repayments per month go up but you are not relying solely on the capital growth of the property to pay off the debt when you eventually sell the property.

Additionally, with principle and interest repayments you are reducing the debt and exposure to that debt. Eventually you may not even need to sell the property, you can simply live off the rental income from the property with no cost of debt against it. The more properties in this situation, the better. Remember to focus on reducing the non-tax deductible debt on your home as a priority. To break with tradition, this does not necessarily have to be done prior to reducing the debt against your investment properties. It all depends on your situation.

RULE:

Over many years, whether you fix your rate or leave it as a variable interest rate, research has shown that you will break even and achieve nothing financially different either way.

Loan Assessment:

Always bear in mind the costs associated with buying an investment property.

Lenders will need to see that you have the money to pay the difference between the loan amount and the purchase price plus costs.

Costs include:

- Stamp duty, conveyancer fee, lender costs (these could be application fees, legal costs, or sometimes valuation), possibly lenders' mortgage insurance.

'The process involved in applying for a loan' diagram shows each step of what happens when applying for a loan. I will make some comments on some of the steps that are less self-explanatory.

Whilst the first step includes contacting a lender or a broker, the reference to contacting a lender would only apply if you simply want to increase your loan on your current facility, but other than that my suggestion still stands, never go directly to a lender.

My previous book, 'Property Finance Made Simple' will prepare you for what you need to provide to your broker for your loan application to be assessed more simply and quickly.

Credit checks are done whenever you apply for a credit card, interest free terms on a lounge suite purchase or similar, and every time you apply for a loan. The more you do this, the more you're a danger to yourself. The danger is becoming less palatable to a lender. Use a broker to compare options for you.

Loan assessment can take a matter of hours or weeks, depending on the lender. Don't rely on an answer from a lender one day before you want to go to auction. Do not apply for finance after bidding at auction or entering into negotiations on a property, as this is just mad. Always have a 'subject to finance' clause in a purchase contract if you can. Of course, you cannot have this if you are successful at auction.

A pre-approval as opposed to a conditional approval, is where the lender assesses everything to make you finance ready to find a property. Pre-approvals can be valid for 30 to 180 days. Ensure your finance clause does not expire prior to a valuation being done by the lender, on the property.

Valuation can be a computer generated one or the valuer may want to visit the property. The lender will decide. This can take a few hours or over a week, longer if there are plans and permits in place on the property.

From formal approval to the documents stage, being ready can take a few hours to perhaps two days. Once documents are returned the lender may normally require 24-48 hours to settle, unless there is a refinance involved. This can take more time as the outgoing lender that you are refinancing away from can often drag their feet to make more money on your loan, just because they can.

From submission of the loan to settlement can be as quick as a week, but normally it would take 3-6 weeks, depending on the lender.

Loan Mortgage Insurance (LMI)

Most lenders, will mortgage insure their loans above 80% loan to value ratio (LVR).

LMI may be able to be added on top of the loan. If you wish to avoid LMI you will have to use more of your cash or equity. Borrowing more for investment properties gives you more tax-deductible interest to claim, it uses less of your own money by having a higher gearing/leverage ratio, and it could help you purchase more properties (depending on the overall cost of debt).

You should consider having a balanced approach as to whether you have a larger loan or higher loan to value ratio, as they will impact on your borrowing capacity and cost to maintain the debt. The higher you leverage yourself the less equity in the property (riskier if the market has a downturn). Compare this to using more of your cash or equity reserves. While this will lead to less money or equity being available for future property purchases, it will contribute to the property being more positively geared.

Commercial Property Finance

Standard residential and commercial lenders will only lend up to 75% generally, as a maximum, and up to 2.5 million for a commercial investment property. Whilst a 15-year term is more common, 30 years is also possible. Lenders have dedicated lending teams for commercial property due to the bespoke nature of the industry, and the diversity in economic conditions that may come to bear on a credit decision. The biggest difference with commercial finance is that it does not fall into a predefined set of boxes as easily as residential lending, it is less predictable.

The type of documentation required is similar to a residential loan, whether low documentation or full documentation, however, with commercial lending, future cash flow forecasts can be considered rather than the black and white approach of residential lending.

Repayment frequency can be the same as residential lending, so weekly, fortnightly, or monthly, with additional repayments allowed, on fixed rates though it is only monthly repayments allowed normally. There is often an 'early termination' fee attached to the loan. Some lenders do provide unlimited cash out to 75% LVR, and this can also be used for working capital and purchase of business equipment.

Stay tuned for my new book 'The 100k Property Plan', which will be quite comprehensive.

RULE:

A finance strategy is as important as a property strategy, making use of lenders as and when they suit your needs.

5

Research and Locate

Compare Data

Gather Data

Dwelling/ Demographic Cohesion

RESEARCH & LOCATE

Street

Supply and Demand

Suburb

State

First let's consider the basics.

You have a plan, with the required number of properties in it and what each one looks like. You have a strategy; it could be buy and hold or renovate/developer and flip. It could be capital growth or cash flow or a balance of both from the same property.

Properties may include a house, townhouse, unit, apartment, villa, terrace, dual occupancy, land, and multiples of these depending on the strategy.

The strategies are broken down into two key aims or needs, growth and cash flow. These are needs that you have to meet between now and your ultimate goal of a comfortable retirement. As discussed, budget, affordability and your tailored plan will influence the following choices.

1. The State within Australia that you purchase each property in;
2. Metro or regional

Then:

1. Metro 1: within 10km of the CBD
2. Metro 2: within 20km of the CBD
3. Metro 3: within 30km of the CBD
4. Fringe: 30km–40km of the CBD
5. Metro: satellite cities/growing hubs
6. Regional hubs

Rule:

Avoid what many investors do. Many investors are drawn towards innuendo, media hype, and listening to friends, family, and backyard self-acclaimed experts, and worse, property marketing companies and real estate agents.

The real issue, which inadvertently leads to failure, lies in not undertaking proper research.

There is no real rulebook out there, until now …

Here are some respectable and risk-reducing considerations that should make your job easier in finding an outperforming location. This also reinforces why it is important to seek objective advice.

Research must be based on facts and figures, and reliable information – unbiased information. This goes for information provided to the investor, and the information the investor is basing their own decision on, as well. Often property investors can fall into the trap of using their own emotion, beliefs, attitude, and experiences to base decisions on, such as where to buy and what to buy, and the inclusions in the property itself. What you or I personally prefer has no relevance when compared to what the area suggests is needed, in reference to the type of dwelling more suitable to the demographic.

Check the position that state is in, in regards to the property cycle – property cycle refers to the period of time over which the price of a property changes by being influenced from demographic, economic and supply and demand changes in the area; each area may have its own cycle and be at different stages than any other area – and whether it is at the bottom, middle, or top of the cycle. It is always a good time to buy, but not everywhere, at any given time.

The peak would be 12 o'clock on a clock (end of the boom), 6 o'clock would be trough (bottom of the market). Between 12 o'clock and 3 o'clock is a correction, 3-5 must avoid, 5-9 is opportunity. It is difficult to know when the top or bottom is going to be 6 o'clock to consider jumping in. Between 11 and 12 o'clock you might want to exercise caution.

Looking at supply and demand in conjunction with population migration is one of the most important points. An example of an area to avoid is Docklands in Melbourne, with the oversupply issues and extremely high vacancy rates. If, however, you look at population migration in isolation you may be led to believe it is a perfect area, hence why it is so important to review population with supply.

If people were not attracted to the area, the area would unlikely increase in value. The fundamental figures start with supply and demand, like any commodity. If there is no demand, then it has little true value.

The more important element of the location is its infrastructure. Some infrastructure is merely 'being discussed' by council, and other authorities, as to 'whether it will be planned'. Then it may end up 'being planned', and move forward to being a 'committed plan'. Once the infrastructure has actually commenced, you can be certain that it is in full swing and it will have a tangible end result. The best solution here is to select a location where there are several existing industries. Be careful if you're acting on something that is only being discussed. It needs to be approved.

You must avoid one-industry towns, because if government contracts cease or spending there ceases and the population is very small, the town will probably die, capital values will drop and vacancy rates will rocket up.

The economy of an area and surrounds, including the amenities there already (and in the pipeline), are important to know. Properties in suburbs with train stations tend to grow more than suburbs without stations in metropolitan locations. Hospitals, schools, other transport, and shops are important too.

The demographics, particularly for guiding you in making a more informed decision about the 'what' you should buy in the area, are very important for your budget, growth, rental, and any works needed on the property, and whether those renovations will improve the value. It also tells you the number of renters in an area. In some areas, units and townhouses are more popular and will have appeal to a greater percentage of the population. In other areas, duplexes or houses are better.

The number of renters versus owners will impact on the upkeep and future desirability of pockets within a suburb.

Vacancy rates (and not just the current rates, but how they are trending) will help you see if the area is becoming more popular, or losing people. A simple snapshot will not demonstrate this, as it only captures a moment in time. When you look at shares you would normally look at trends, so do the same with property.

This methodology applies to the following points: Capital growth history, yields, days on the market, discounting and auction clearance rates, median house prices, population, supply and demand, vacancy rates, stock on market, income and employment growth is also very important.

Many people think that when a property has been on the market for two months nobody wants it (many people do not invest wisely though). I see opportunity. Maybe the vendor has been out of touch with reality of what the property is really worth. The agent normally has signed a three-month contract to sell it, both the vendor and agent may be more pliable and agreeable to a lower price. Look at the best streets; try to stay within a couple of blocks of these streets.

Comparable sales and timing of these is very handy and vital to your negotiations. You can compare what similar properties sold for within the previous six months, within three months is better (this is what valuers and financial institutions use) and use this as ammunition; it also provides you confidence in what the property may be worth. Sales within 1km is best, others in the same suburb may still be okay if a little further away. Comparing land size within 10% or less variance, and compare the same number of bedrooms and bathrooms – there is software that will do all this for you.

If new: Just focusing on fittings and fixtures included in the property, quality, uniqueness is good but be aware of what other properties in the estate include.

Oversupply, master-planned communities, and excess land can all hinder growth. Prime examples could be suburbs in growth corridors; there could be better opportunities to be had further in towards the CBD/town centre. In some of these large estates, schools, hospitals, shopping centres, and a train station may improve your property. Trains and access to transport are big factors in the investment being viable.

There is software out there, which allows you to drill down in a suburb and overlay your own preferences to find an ideal location within a suburb.

Figures suggest choosing the street wisely can deliver much more capital growth than the rest of the suburb, rather than just haphazardly buying in a suburb, and it is a low percentage of a suburb where ideal streets lie. You may wish to understand which streets have less public housing and streets where people earn more than other streets. Rent and yield is higher on some streets, and you can avoid streets with too many units or apartments, and understand which streets have too high a percentage of tenants versus owner occupiers.

Of course, a good buyer's agent will have access to several software programs that on aggregate may cost a significant amount per year to subscribe to. Leveraging off a buyer's agent and their access to data and knowledge in combining all the data, can save you thousands in annual subscriptions for the same outcome, not to mention hundreds of thousands in buying the right versus wrong property.

Even then, doing it on your own is fraught with danger, without leveraging off the experience and knowledge of the buyer's agent.

The next diagram shows the flow of steps that should be followed when undertaking research. This is an unemotional process, in order to maximise results.

Here is the crucial process of sourcing a good property

Median House Price

Median price can often be misleading and unreliable. Half the properties in a suburb are under the median price and half are over. Sometimes buyers think if they can buy under median they're doing well. Often the contrary is the case. It is not enough just to buy in a good suburb, although this is 75-80% of the work done, but it is important to buy in a good street in the suburb. The best streets in a suburb outperform the average and certainly outperform the worst streets.

Of course, it is worth mentioning that if you purchase under the median, of a better street or pocket of the suburb you are acquiring more capital growth potential from the start.

Be very careful also of a false median. When new stock in an area comes onto the market or land has been carved up and two or three townhouses built on it, this can lead to sales of property in the area with prices way above the median. The sales prices can lead novice buyers to believe there has been significant capital growth in the area, when in fact prices may not have even risen. What could have happened is one of many things. For example:

1. A newer property has sold for more than an older property.
2. Larger parcels of land, or development sites may have been sold.

Of course, don't rely too heavily on the median price for a suburb for one more very important reason; the suburb is comprised of different sized dwellings.

Size can be:

1. Number of bedrooms
2. Size of each bedroom
3. Number of living areas
4. Number of bathrooms
5. Size of land
6. Garage versus carport
7. Quality of inclusions is another consideration.

So median can come back by a third or half in one month then double in another.

At a bare minimum, only ever use the median price of the particular size dwelling you are trying to buy, as a starting point, never the median for the suburb. Compare apples with apples in other words.

So look at three-bedroom house and four bedroom house medians separately, for example. This provides a more accurate guide as to what you would expect to pay for the same size dwelling. Accompanied by an online valuation containing comparable sales, this can be used to make a more informed decision as to what to offer at auction or what to pay during negotiations. It also allows you to compare the capital growth and yield based on a specific number of bedrooms to see which is more popular in the suburb, besides looking at the demographics of the area.

The more popular the dwelling size the easier it may rent, as there's more demand – ensuring you understand what the supply is in comparison to the demand of course.

Commercial Property

In Australia more than five million people are employed by over two million small to medium enterprises. Source (ABS). The industry is growing rapidly and exceeds 400 billion as of 2016.

The biggest difference with this market and the residential market is the fact that more macro and Government policy conditions affect the commercial space. Economic as distinct from market conditions can vary across commercial property grades and regions. Commercial property is riskier when it comes to vacancy. More macro level classifications apply to commercial property, more so than residential. Entire sectors can be affected at any one time in an entire region, rather than being more centric to a particular suburb. Tourist accommodation, retail property, office and industrial can all suffer in an entire region.

The problem with commercial property is its inherent lack of long-term, stable growth – just like the stock market, which is directly linked to the corporate world.

Many experts say that there is a high percentage of business failure in the first two years. Dunn & Bradstreet research shows that more than 80% of business failures are related to cash flow (rather than sales pressures). Vacancy rates can be high which soon offset the previously accompanying higher yields, so yields now are no longer taken for granted as being at 8%, they can be around 5-6% quite often.

Commercial property may include a business, shop, retail, resort-style offices, factories, farms, multi-unit developments, warehouses, industrial units, mixed residential and commercial use, and income-producing properties. The list goes on.

The values of the properties concerned are based on the rental returns. Often the tenant pays all the outgoings (i.e. insurance, rates, and fit out). This is a different market and requires different knowledge and due diligence.

Strata offices are becoming popular as people can rent them close to where they live, and it allows them to escape the distractions and interruptions at home, and expand their business at the same time. (Strata title refers to a situation where the individual/entity owns part of the property such as the dwelling, i.e. townhouse, unit or office, but they share ownership of the rest of the property such as some or all of the land, driveways, gardens, foyers, corridors in apartment buildings etc. Normally more than two dwellings that share a drive or common land require a body corporate/owners corporation to be established to insure the land and manage the responsibility of the shared areas. Caravan parks, resorts, retirement villages are more obvious examples of this.)

Constructing more than three dwellings on one title would normally require a commercial loan.

For your own free copy of my own personal comprehensive research checklist, please go to my website www. australianpropertyadvisorygroup.com.au/resources.

This checklist covers most things that should be considered when researching, there are instructions on the checklist of how best to use it.

RULE:

If you follow this process, you will dramatically enhance your ability to time the market better, take more advantage of out-performing potential, reduce the risk, and balance the effect on your lifestyle – and better your future.

6

Purchase

Now you have found a property, or your buyer's agent has found a property or short list of properties for you that suit your plan and property strategy. They have been well researched, finance is pre-approved, you have decided on a conveyancer to use and you have a property inspector in mind. You have spoken to your accountant to advise you if you should purchase the property in your own name or in the name of another entity, such as a company or a trust. Upon deciding which property you want to purchase, you either attend the auction if there is one, or you start negotiating.

Auction

If the property is going to auction, it is important to consider a few important things.

Are you confident to bid on your own, or do you require a buyer's agent to bid for you? There are many games that are played at auctions and you need to understand the rules of the game.

You need to decide on the maximum price you're prepared to bid, and be prepared to walk away.

If you win at auction you need to have understood whether it is 5% or 10% you pay on the day by internet transfer, evidencing receipt of payment to the agent or bank cheque. You cannot change your mind. There is no cooling off period.

You cannot have a clause in the contract of 'subject to finance' nor 'subject to property and pest inspection'. This leaves you awfully exposed and dramatically increases the risk for you.

What if you pay too much for the property? You may not think it's too much but what you think does not matter as much as what a valuer will think. I have seen situations where someone is happy with the price they paid, and they attempt to convince the lender of that, but instead of the valuation coming in at contract price it comes back $50k or even a $150k under. A $750k property being valued at $580k is an example of what I have seen. The likelihood of this happening is greater if you have not used a good buyer's agent or you have purchased from a property marketing company spruiker (alias your enemy).

If it was a new property then it would not be an auction, but the same risk of paying too much applies. People often say the property is worth what someone is prepared to pay; normally the real estate agent says this as a flippant and quite ignorant throwaway line. You won't be so compliant with this way of thinking if you lose your 5-10% deposit because you cannot settle on the property.

What if the property has some major defects or many smaller but expensive issues you need to resolve upon purchasing it?

So, what can you do to try and reduce some of the risk?

You can pay for a property inspection to be done prior to auction, understanding of course, that you risk having wasted $380, if you are unsuccessful at auction. A further $200-$300 could be wasted if a pest inspection was also done. What a great insurance policy in a way, it at least would provide comfort in bidding at auction; it is a small price to pay to help avoid making perhaps a several hundred-thousand-dollar mistake

Ensure you have a pre-approval in place before auction, this does not do anything to eliminate the risk of a low valuation or you paying too much, but at least the risk of not even getting finance is reduced.

You just cannot change the fact though that you can't have a 'subject to finance clause' in the contract.

You could also try buying the property before auction. Some vendors will accept an offer, some want the offer to be a crazy offer, and others may simply accept a reasonable offer to avoid the risk of the property not selling at auction. If the vendor does accept an offer from you, you could negotiate to have the clauses inserted in the contract.

> ### RULE:
>
> *You cannot have a 'subject to finance' clause or 'subject to property and pest inspection' clause in the contract under auction conditions, you are not protected.*

Private treaty

With a private treaty, i.e. when a property is not going to auction, you can insert the clauses in the contract, subject to negotiations. Be wary of dodgy real-estate agents. One example is a property in Frankston, Victoria. The agent was willing to accept a finance clause but not a property inspection clause in the contract. This has problems written all over it and it would more than likely suggest that the agent knows there is a problem and lacks the integrity to tell you. In this case we walked away and later discovered there were in fact serious issues with the property. If you think you can always trust the sales agent, think again.

When there is a private treaty, different agents have different ways of handling the process.

In March 1999, the office of fair-trading released a video of the president of the REIQ stating, *'We have a legal, moral and fiduciary duty to promote and protect the interests of the vendor and have no interest in the purchaser.'*

There are several approaches the can agents take, and you need to ascertain which approach is the one you must follow.

1. You submit a tender, putting your best foot forward and the agent presents all offers to the vendor. No second chance, this does not provide you the ability to negotiate, and you risk offering more than you may have needed to, or too little.
2. You can negotiate with some back and forth until either

you walk away because the vendor still wants more, or you agree on a price. This process can be via email if in NSW, leading to an offer being submitted on a signed contract and presented to the vendor. If the agent asks you if you're willing to fill in a contract it suggests you are close, but not in Victoria. In Victoria, many agents will not want to waste their time with you until you submit any offer on a signed contract. In my soon to be published book, ('The 100k Property Plan; how to earn $100,000 per year from property') I will go into depth on differences between different states of Australia. Each state is different.

3. Once you sign the contract in a private treaty situation it is normal to have seven days for property and pest inspection to be carried out, and 21 days for finance to be fully approved (in Victoria). In NSW for example you may only have seven days for property and pest, and 14 days for finance in general. In Victoria, you may have 30, 60 or 90 days agreed settlement period, sometimes 120 days. You could even negotiate 12 months, with access to the property prior, for your personal enjoyment. In NSW, it is 42 days. Again, other states will be covered in my next book.

7

Team

Buyer's Agent/
Property Advisor

Broker

Property
Inspector

Accountant

YOUR TEAM

Conveyancer

Quantity
Surveyor

Building and
Landlord Insurance
Options

The importance of having a team around you cannot be overstated. No one has enough knowledge to wear every hat needed in a property purchase situation. It is naïve for anyone to think they can do it all themselves. I will list the team in order of when you need them; some will naturally overlap, as it is not a perfect sequence.

RULE:

Use a good conveyancer/lawyer, one that will help you fill in the contract. A lawyer is often better as they can provide legal advice. A conveyancer, unless they are a lawyer, is limited in the advice they can provide.

1. Accountant

Make sure yours has initiative. Even more importantly, ensure that they specialise in investment property, or at least have adequate knowledge.

Benefits of an accountant are as follows:

1. Determination of whether you buy in a trust name, company name or your own name.
2. If in your own name, determination of the percentage of ownership split between all purchasers. Given the higher income earner will normally pay more tax, if you have someone not earning an income with a high percentage of ownership on title you could be paying unnecessary tax.
3. Help avoid purchasing too many negatively geared properties, as there could be no tax advantages in holding more than one or two negatively geared properties, as it could place their income below the tax-free threshold and result in a negative outcome.
4. Correctly determine how any costs for renovations be apportioned. Many people make the mistake of incorrectly claiming costs in their first tax return rather than the costs being apportioned as capital costs.

5. A good accountant can ensure you don't miss out on claimable items for extra tax deductions.
6. The accountant will help you look after your investment property, which is best done from day one, by minimising holding costs and helping ensure the property is more affordable.
7. They help you plan your money more effectively in order to have a balance with your property ownership and any changing interest rates and the effect of the interest rate on the property. I've seen people buy in a company, but not realise there are absolutely no capital gains tax concessions. At least in their personal name they are entitled to a 50% tax concession on capital gains tax, if they own the property for more than 12 months.

Many people do not realise that by being entitled to claim depreciation on the property, they will end up paying more capital gains tax when they sell. Notice I say, 'entitled to' whether they claim depreciation or not, they will pay more capital gains tax if there were any claimable depreciable items during ownership of the property. Depreciating the building reduces the value of the building, which in turn widens the gap between its depreciated value and the sale price.

A quality property is not just about it doubling in value but it's also about not having a property that is costing you an arm and a leg. Accountants can assist you with preparing a profit and loss schedule, and a PAYG withholding variation (if applicable).

Do not use an accountant that receives kickbacks from referring you to someone selling properties – that accountant is no better that the dastardly spruiker.

2. Broker

1. A broker saves you time.
2. They compare banks' borrowing capacity calculators, to determine which will lend you the most and will offer you

the most favourable interest rate and lowest fees. Fees and rates can be compared online easily enough but borrowing capacity calculators cannot be compared as easily, so why waste your time doing this when a broker will do it for free.

3. A bank employee lacks the knowledge, diversity, depth of experience and range of products and solutions to add any real value to you in building a property portfolio.

4. Package up the deal, track its progress, and do all the leg work for you.

3. Buyer's Agent and Property Advisor

1. A buyer's agent takes all the legwork out of finding a property. You need a buyer's agent specialising in helping investors. This involves a different set of criteria to find the best property for you to invest in, rather than finding a property to live in.

2. As buyer's agents, we often meet people who unfortunately have trusted a real estate agent when buying an established property, or they have trusted a property marketing company when buying a new property.

Rule:

Buyer's agents represent the buyer. Real estate agents and property marketing companies represent the seller. DO NOT trust a real estate agent when buying an established property, or a property marketing company when buying a new or established property.

3. Research and due diligence are the most important things to undertake when buying an investment property. Knowing which areas to buy in for capital growth or for cash flow around Australia. Use a buyer's agent not limited to one state or one property type or strategy is important for all investors. It's important to have a balanced approach to capital growth and cash flow, reducing the likelihood of running out of equity for your next purchase or borrowing capacity with a bank.

4. When considering investing, so often people don't appreciate the time it takes to find the right property. They end up going around in circles, trying to sift through the seemingly limitless choices available, whilst actually not really understanding or appreciating there are very few properties that are considered investment grade properties. Often you will end up going to many open house inspections, then perhaps an auction, or negotiation, only then to miss out, and do it all again, spending hours on an online portal. So use a buyer's agent.

5. People need to understand what street the property is on, what it's near to, aspect, size, layout, yield, tenant demand, supply and demand, covenants on the property. They should then have a property inspection that could highlight potential issues which could lead you to pull out of the contract and start the process all over again. You need to consider the settlement period, terms of agreement and clauses as well. A buyer's agent can negotiate for you or bid at auction for you, which could save you the same if not more than the buyer's agent fee, compared to negotiating yourself.

6. Leverage off invaluable knowledge and experience, identifying the next potential hotspot.

7. Access to properties that you may have never known about.

RULE:

Whether established property, new, house, townhouse, unit, cash flow, capital growth, inner city, regional, interstate, buy and hold or develop or flip, use a buyer's agent.

4. Conveyancer

Conveyancing tends to be an afterthought when buying property, however buyers can reduce the risk of their buying decision by consulting a conveyancer or solicitor before they sign a contract. They provide a practical approach to the buying process by not only alerting the buyer to potential traps and risks in the buying process but also in the undertaking of more effective due diligence when having found a property.

You must get your conveyancer to read over the contract before you sign it, and they must be licensed in the state in which the property is in, most are only licensed in one state.

They will ensure your rights are as protected as possible, such as having a subject to property and pest inspection, and a subject to finance clause.

With the property inspection clause, it is often written such as 'subject to no major structural defects' Seek advice to include the following, 'subject to the buyer's satisfaction', although this could be construed as too vague for the vendor. It just depends if the sales agent picks up on it, often I have had it sail through.

You may consider not dating the contract when signing. This can buy more time between when you sign it and when the vendor signs the contract, as usually the clauses commence from the date of contract. This is often better if it is a later date than the day the buyer signs the contract. Try to insert a clause in the contract allowing access to the property up to 2-3 weeks prior to settlement for tenants to be shown through by the property manager you have engaged.

Other important reasons to use them include, but not limited to:

1. Timely settlement to avoid penalties charged by the vendor.
2. Any problems with p/work, title, contract, documents etc., are more likely to be addressed appropriately and in a timely fashion.
3. Determination of entitlements, any adjustments for costs, such as rates, water etc., so no liability travels with the property.
4. Assistance with the completion of forms.
5. Communication between the lender/broker, and the vendor and conveyance firm representing the vendor.

6. Titles registered correctly, in the correct ownership structure and correct ownership percentages.

7. Determination and advice on any negative or limiting factors or factors the buyer should be aware of such as; Environmental limitations, covenants, easements, boundaries, caveats.

5. Property inspector

Arrange property and pest inspection once vendors have signed contract. Their fee may be around $400-$600.

Property Inspections

Normally you have seven days from signing a purchase contract for a property and pest inspection to be carried out, but only if you inserted this clause in the purchase contract.

An independent building inspection is not only the smart thing to do, it is vitally important.

An agent's 30 minute 'open for inspection' is not enough time for prospective purchasers to inspect the most important areas of a home, the subfloor, roof space and roof.

The subfloor may reveal numerous issues in a home that unless revealed prior to a purchase may cost a lot of money:

1. Dead animals
2. Mould on the ground
3. Damp ground
4. Water ponding
5. Rotting timber stumps
6. Concrete stumps reduced in size from concrete cancer
7. Ducted heating ducts disconnected
8. Subfloor timbers cut to accommodate bathroom wastes
9. Lack of subfloor ventilation
10. Asbestos
11. Leaking showers causing mould or rot to timber and flooring
12. Owners building rubbish and or belongings
13. Termites.

And worst of all:

- No access point to inspect.

The roof space may also reveal numerous issues:

1. Lack of ceiling insulation or insulation is aged and ineffective
2. Old unused gravity feed hot water systems
3. Old asbestos heater flues
4. Vermin or signs of mice, rats, possums, birds
5. Cracked roof tiles
6. Owner's belongings and/or rubbish.

The roof and gutter:

1. Blocked gutters
2. Cracked roof tiles
3. Cracked roof tile bedding mortar
4. Weathered timbers, gables and fascias
5. Leaking flashings
6. Owners belongings, e.g. balls in gutters.

The report will identify whether any defects are a major or minor, and whether in fact they pose a safety issue and will be a handy reference if you do purchase the property; especially if future maintenance is required.

All new homes have a seven-year warranty period; however, the warranty for some components of new homes diminishes over time. A report can identify which items are still covered at any time during the subsequent seven-year period. Do not blindly rely on this warranty though. All new constructions require a building surveyor to be engaged by the builder to provide inspections on up to three of the five build stages, normally, slab, frame and final stage. The inspections are often limited with less regard for quality of work and owner's specifications. Often, they miss a number of things that are done that may not be to standard or code, such as plumbing and waterproofing, insulation not to requirements, and many other serious shortcomings. I have seen so many complete failings by dodgy builders; some are just a complete disgrace.

Ensure you insert in your contract that a property inspector working for you, not the builder, inspects all work being undertaken.

Don't let presentation of a property distract you from looking for underlying defects.

Some defects may be of a minor nature but if left unattended could result in costly and time-consuming repairs in the future.

RULE:

Property inspections are necessary for every property; you cannot just blindly trust the quality of the builder or their finished product.

Pest inspection is also advisable for the following reasons:

1. To identify if there are any pests present, in particular, termites.
2. If conditions are the sort of environment that pests would like.
3. Pest inspections may not be necessary for brand new properties.

Rule:

Never blindly trust a builder, you must verify his work. Never trust a real estate agent or vendor, you must verify the state of the dwelling with an established property as much as a new property.

6. Rental manager

Eight weeks out from handover of new property, or four weeks from settlement of an established property, start discussions with a rental manager. You could negotiate to have early access to an established property to allow the rental manager to show people around if there isn't already a tenant in there. Whilst you may think the vendor would not like this, not every sale and purchase is perfect for both sides there is always compromise, this may be a compromise a vendor will accept, especially in a buyer's market.

It may be easier to engage the firm that the sales agent works for as they still have the keys and they may already know the property quite well. They may not be your preferred choice but let's be pragmatic here. Use them until settlement then ditch them after settlement and hand the reins over to your preferred rental manager. Business is business, so if you think someone else will do a better job then go for it. You owe no loyalty to the sales firm, they represent the seller. Remember, they are the ones who have negotiated against you for you to pay more.

When choosing a rental agent, always look for:

1. A well-established company with a good and well established or well experienced rental management team.
2. Ensure the commission paid is well spent. This is generally 6- 8% plus GST for their management fee to collect rent and one to two weeks' rent for leasing. If you have two or three properties with one agent you may be able to negotiate down to 5% plus GST. Always avoid companies that only have one property manager, it is incredibly frustrating when you cannot get hold of them, and they always seem to be out of the office, and if they are off for the day, well, too bad, there is no solution for you. This is no way to run a business, and you should not have to deal with such a firm. Some companies just have really lame and/or unprofessional practices.

7. Quantity surveyor

Investors should always, always obtain a depreciation schedule. This is required for taxation purposes if you wish to try and save some tax. If you do not wish to save tax then refer to the quote from Kerry Packer.

This should be obtained as soon as possible, certainly prior to you submitting your next tax return after the purchase.

A quantity surveyor places a depreciable value on the building. It of course excludes the land value component of the purchase price, and they place a value on the fittings and fixtures in the dwelling. You will need to provide them the purchase price and construction price (if applicable).

Of course, you can no longer claim depreciation on fittings and fixtures on an established property, nor on a dwelling built prior to September 1987.

8. Building and landlord insurance options

Building and landlord insurance options should commence at least by the day before or day of handover. Your bank may require the certificate of currency be provided prior to handover/settlement, and would normally have to be at a value determined by the replaceable value figure provided by the valuer.

The cost of landlord insurance can range from $220 per annum upwards and perhaps closer to $1000 for building insurance; more in QLD given the regular floods they seem to receive.

Choose wisely between landlord insurance providers to ensure you are receiving adequate protection. Bear in mind that if the property does have owner's corporation fees associated with it, this would typically include in the premium the building insurance cover, not landlord insurance cover.

Consider obtaining common ground insurance if buying any property, which does share common ground.

FINAL WORD

You have almost come to the end of my handbook, and I am sure you have been able to take a great deal of benefit from having read my book. As the title suggests, there will be an updated version released every two years with any necessary changes, advances in methodology and action packed with more insights aimed at helping you start and/or continue to grow your portfolio. Property investing is a journey – it should be an enjoyable, stress free journey.

The most important thing you could take away is balance. Without balance in a property portfolio, it will be difficult to grow a portfolio of adequate size to suit your future needs, without negatively impacting on the present and near future. We have to live life for today and live life with tomorrow in mind.

This book has been about what you need to do every time you purchase a property. My next book will be building on this and based on what you need to do to grow a property portfolio to earn $100,000 a year income from property.

Contact

If you would like assistance with buyer advocacy, property advice, or being put in contact with a suitably qualified professional offering one of the services of those listed in chapter 7 please contact us.

To obtain a copy of my *Blueprint to Property Investment Success*, *go to the following link.*

www.australianpropertyadvisorygroup.com.au/resources

Additionally, you may wish to purchase one of my other books for $14.99 instead of $24.99

Property Investing Made Simple

Property Finance Made Simple

If you quote 'discount18' you will receive 5% off on our buyer advocacy or property advisory services

WEBSITES

www.propertyinvestingmadesimple.com.au

www.propertyfinancemadesimple.net.au

www.australianpropertyadvisorygroup.com.au

RESOURCES

The 'readiness to invest questionnaire', my blueprint ©, and your own research checklist, please visit my website.

www.australianpropertyadvisorygroup.com.au/resources

EMAIL

advice@australianpropertyadvisorygroup.com.au

or

Andrew@apag.com.au

PHONE

1300 760901

www.facebook.com/australianpropertyadvisorygroup

www.facebook.com/propertyfinancemadesimple/

www.facebook.com/Propertyinvestingmadesimple/

www.twitter.com/CrossleyAndrew

https://www.linkedin.com/in/andrewccrossley/

Printed in Australia
AUHW021022090221
340939AU00010B/18

9 781925 692211